50 Years
of
Cats and Dogs

PETS WE LOVED AND CARED FOR

BY BILL HORNE

Archway Publishing books may be ordered through booksellers or by contacting:

Archway Publishing
1663 Liberty Drive
Bloomington, IN 47403
www.archwaypublishing.com
844-669-3957

Because of the dynamic nature of the Internet, any web addresses or links contained in this book may have changed since publication and may no longer be valid. The views expressed in this work are solely those of the author and do not necessarily reflect the views of the publisher, and the publisher hereby disclaims any responsibility for them.

Any people depicted in stock imagery provided by Getty Images are models, and such images are being used for illustrative purposes only.
Certain stock imagery © Getty Images.

ISBN: 978-1-6657-3547-6 (sc)
ISBN: 978-1-6657-3548-3 (e)

Library of Congress Control Number: 2022923490

Print information available on the last page.

Archway Publishing rev. date: 02/09/2023

Contents

Peppy, Borderline Border Collie

Peppy was a maverick. We bought a new house and barely moved in and settled down, when this maverick dog showed up.

Our property was completely fenced in with gates for entry to the walkway and driveway. Because of our three-year-old son, we kept all gates closed so he could have access to the yard. This maverick dog would never attempt to come in the yard or leave the neighborhood.

One day, our neighbor's child was playing with this wayward dog and she bit the child. Because we were new in the neighborhood, the neighbor thought the dog belonged to us. When we were notified of the dog bite, my wife offered to take her to the doctor and have her checked. The neighbor advised my wife that the skin was not broken and invited her in for a cup of coffee. The (good) thing about the dog bite? This started a friendship that lasted for over 40 years.

You guessed it. From that day on, the wayward dog was no longer wayward. She became the Horne's dog and we named her Peppy. We then carried Peppy to the Vet to have her shots updated. When we returned home, we placed her inside the gated fence and forbade her to ever go outside.

It did not take long to find out Peppy was highly intelligent. We had no way of knowing her age. We knew she was not a puppy. So, I started teaching her several tricks and she caught on very quickly. Some of the things are listed below.

A, shake hands (after all don't all animals learn that)
B. Sit (same as above)
C. Play dead
D. Love my feet
E. Retrieve items

The neat thing she always did that I did not teach her was, every time I came home from work or other places, she would run to another part of the yard as if she was chasing someone or some intruder.

One day we got a new postman. We always had our mailbox on the fence facing outward so the mail carrier would not have to come in. After all, she had already bit the neighbor's child.

This mail carrier began kicking the fence to get Peppy roweled up. I came home from work one evening, my wife told me of this going on. I could not believe that a grown man, with a responsible job, would do such a thing.

I came home for lunch one day and I heard Peppy barking to the top of her sound box. I went to the door and I saw this mail carrier kicking the fence. I yelled to him, "If you kick that fence one more time, I will open that gate and turn her loose on you." That ended the fence kicking by USPS. However, it was too late. She already had his looks stamped into her memory bank.

As my son grew older, he also grew bolder. He saw the mail carrier coming he opened the gate. And when he reached our mail box, he met his worst night mare and Peppy did not bite him but she chewed up his trouser leg.

The next day I receive a phone call from the Post Master Informing me that I had to tie Peppy up during the mail delivery time or we would not receive mail.

I am a very patient man and very seldom get angry. When he finished his dialogue with me, I began to let him know what kind of scum he had as a mail carrier. I explained how this mail carrier intimidated Peppy and she was waiting for the day of revenge to come. We came to a mutual agreement and life continued on without further incidents.

Five years passed and we bought a home in the neighborhood we always wanted to live. Peppy was a tamed and friendly dog and did not bother strangers. Not even mail carriers.

My wife's mother and father lived on the next street over and down the block a little way.

We would now and then walk over to see them. Peppy would sometime follow us over. When I had to work on the weekend, my wife and the boys would walk to Church. The church where we worshiped was about three blocks from where her mom lived.

Peppy knew the route well. There would be times when peppy would not be in the yard and my wife would call her mom and ask If Peppy was there and she would be in the swing with Nanny. After a little while she would be told to go home and she would obey. Peppy would not follow my wife and boys to the church building, but would be outside by the entrance door waiting for service to end.

Peppy was a good dog. One of the smartest canines I have ever seen. However, she had a bad and dangerous habit, chasing cars and nipping at the tires. On November 6, 1968, while nipping at the tires of the Waste Management truck, she was struck and killed. The driver of the truck knocked on the door and told me what happened and apologized. I assured him it was alright and I was expecting to see that one day due to her nature. He asked if I wanted him to put her on the truck and I replied no. She was too good of a pet to end up in a waste management field.

I carried her into a private place and buried her. As I was digging her grave, I had tears streaming down my face. I thought of all the times I asked her to play dead and she would immediately roll over. Well, she will never have to perform that trick again except maybe in my memory. I loved Peppy. We all loved Peppy. Peppy was the first pet that I ever grieved over and to this day 53 years later I still miss her.

CHAPTER TWO

Cinnamon – The Chosen one

My employer at the time of death of Peppy was a National Life Insurance Company. I had several clients and I became close friends with all. At the first of the month, I had to personally contact about 50% of them.

There was this one client that I was not particularly close to but she was always kind and friendly. As I visited, her at the first of the month, she invited me in. When we finished the transaction on her account, she asked if I wanted to see her babies. I was in no hurry that day so I obliged her. We walked to her back yard and there was a new litter of the fuzziest puppies I had ever seen.

This was pretty soon after the death of Peppy and my family was without a pet. She asked if I would be interested in one and I answered quickly with a big yes!

She granted me first pick of the litter and I chose this fuzzy faced female that was separated from the litter doing her own thing. Since the litter was only a few days old, the lady said I could pick her up the following month.

I did not mention this to my wife because it was too soon after the death of Peppy. She gave me the impression she was not interested in another pet to care for and get attached to.

The month passed pretty quick and the time has come to pick up fuzzy face. The friend had her ready for me, cleaned and in a clean card board box. This was about mid-morning and I had to keep the new pet in the box and in the car until evening time when I returned home.

The car had air and I left it running while I was out taking care of business and she was really comfortable all day. Confused and excited, but comfortable.

Finally, the day passes and I arrived home that evening to show off fuzzy face and experience the element of surprise to the family. My wife, the two boys and my mother-in-law were there when I brought the package in. They wanted to know right away the contents of the box.

I explained that I had a surprise in the box for my wife and if she did not want it, I would take it back to where I got it. I reached in and lifted her up and gently put her on the floor. She began running around and having an exciting time in her new home. Finally, I ask my wife if she wanted me to take it back to the lady that gave her to me. I was really surprised at her answer. "You knew if I saw her, I would want to keep her." I was relieved to hear that. She had long honey colored hair and we agreed to name her Cinnamon.

The time of year was the last week of October. Cinnamon was a real quiet dog and slept well at night. She was already potty trained when I picked her up and brought her home for us to keep.

I remember the first time she barked was on Halloween night. Trick or treaters came up to the door and knocked and she let out a bark that was much louder than I would have expected for her age and size. It scared her as if she did not know that the sound would come out of her. I am glad I was there to witness that event.

The following month when I returned to the house where I got Cinnamon from, the lady's husband was there. He wanted to know how Cinnamon was doing and if showed signs of being intelligent. "Oh, yes. I spoke and asked her how much was nine times nine? I told him she barked 81 times. Of course, I was only jesting. He related to me that Cinnamon's mother who was a Scottish Terrier, brought him her food dish and put it at his feet to let him know she was hungry. He went to say he was entertaining company in his den, and he heard this flopping sound coming down the hallway. Pretty soon he found out that it was the dog bringing the food bowl for him to feed her.

Not too long after that the same thing happened to me. I heard this flopping sound coming my way and finally it was Cinnamon bringing her water bowl to me for some water. The DNA of her mother showed up in her.

I began teaching her tricks like I did Peppy. She seemed to have a higher level of intelligence than Peppy because she seemed to learn quicker. One day I heard a dog psychologist on the Mike Douglas TV Show say that dogs were color blind. I did not believe that so I went to F. W. Woolworth store and bought three balls about the size of a tennis ball. There was a red one, blue one and a yellow one. When I returned home, I laid the three balls on the floor about 12 inches apart and sat her down about six feet facing the three balls.

I took a pointer and each time I would touch a ball I would say, Cinnamon, red ball or blue ball or yellow ball. I would do that for several repetitions before I would give the command to retrieve the ball.

When I felt like she was ready, I would take the pointer and say, Cinnamon fetch the red ball, touching the red ball or whatever color I was touching at the time. I don't recall the time frame it took for her to choose the color I wanted and she would retrieve it for me.

I taught her to retrieve things by spelling out where they were. Such as table, I would say, Cinnamon there is a treat on the t-a-b-l-e or c-h-a-l-r.

She was very sensitive to people that had physical impairments. Sometimes my mother would come to stay a few days with us, and wherever she would sit, Cinnamon would sit close to her. Cinnamon would never let anyone get close to her, especially strangers.

Some of the thing she did and was good at were:

a. Play dead
b. Retrieve items
c. Retrieve items by color
d. Retrieve items by spelling them
e. Mouthed the phrase I love you
f. Sing on command

Cinnamon was the smartest pet I ever owned. She loved cream filled donuts and the day she was put to sleep, we let her eat as many donuts she wanted.

She was a friendly pet and let anyone love her. Very child friendly and protective of the elderly. There is a lot more I could say about Cinnamon but the story would not be short.

CHAPTER THREE

Lucky - The Lucky One

After having to put Cinamon to sleep, I was not interested in having any more dogs. Cinamon lived for many years and I had grown so close to her. She was intelligent and could be trained to do anything that dogs could do.

I was so hurt when the decision was made to put her to sleep. As a matter of fact, I was unable to go to the vet when he was going to put her to sleep.

After a few weeks or months passed, as we were eating, our dinner one evening, my wife began to tell me about this dog she had seen and wanted to know if we could adopt him. Seated at the dinner with my wife and I was my two sons. I cannot remember their ages at the time because of the number of years that had passed by.

Naturally, I began to resist the pressure to adopt the little mutt they were trying to describe to me. I was hungry, I had worked all day and I was trying to enjoy my meal. All I could hear was, PLEASE, PLEASE, PLEASE!

Finally, I could not take it any longer and I gave in. What are we going to name him, asked my wife. I suggested Lucky, because he was lucky, I gave in to the pressure.

Lucky was already full grown and did not need any training that a new puppy would require. It was sort of hard for him to settle in the new home provided him.

He had brand new everything to make him comfortable. A new home, a new bed, a new water container with cool water and new toys. Even with all that he wanted to run away every time I opened the door. I mean he ran with wide open speed. I had to get into the car and chase him down and bring him back home.

We had a fenced in back yard with a gate wide enough for adults could walk through with a lawn mower. When we kept the gate closed, he could play in the back yard without getting out. There was an alley behind each house in the community so the police could patrol and keep the homeowners safe from burglaries.

On my way to work every morning I would look down the alley ways to see if anyone was fooling around behind the houses. On my way to work this particular morning I thought I saw a pair of familiar dog ears in the alley. I put the car in reverse and backed up far enough so I could pull into the alley and check these ears and guess what!!!? You guessed it; the ears belonged to Lucky. I scuffed him up and carried him back and found out someone left the gate open and he escaped. He was wet, full of beggar weeds and I was late for work.

Lucky was not a one master dog. He belonged to my wife, my two sons and I was the one that financed his life style as a member of the family. He did not require too much attention. How do you measure how much attention is given to an intelligent dog? Of course, Lucky did not require much attention. However, he received attention from everyone, family members and strangers. He was a friendly dog especially to children.

Lucky began to show his intelligence in his mannerisms and I thought it would be good to see if he was too old to learn new tricks. He was quick to catch on to everything and listed below is a few things I was able teach him successfully.

a. Retrieve sticks, balls, etc.,
b. Dance on his hind legs.
c. Roll over.
d. Play dead.
e. Sing

Lucky really loved riding in the car. Every time I would get the car keys in my hand, he would jump up to the back of my recliner and shake, whine and dance wanting to go for a ride in the car. I would occasionally put him in the car and ride him around the block and that would satisfy him until the next time.

We bought a Tennessee mountain cabin in Cosby, TN. Cosby, TN is 505 miles from Jacksonville Beach, FL where our home is. We carried him with us each time we would go up there for a couple of weeks

Lucky enjoyed traveling in the car. I have always driven four door cars because of the room and space. Even though Lucky had the whole back seat area and a pad to lay on, his desire was to stick his nose close to the A/C when traveling. Also, he loved it when we stopped in the rest area and carried him to the dog walk area.

Our cabin was on a one-acre lot about 500 feet on the side of the mountain in the fork in the road. There were two gravel roads that passed by our cabin. One passed on the side of the cabin and the other passed in front of the cabin.

When I would walk Lucky, I would walk him up the gravel road that passed by the side of the cabin because it was steeper and harder to climb.

One day as we were walking, he stepped off to the side of the road to take care of his business, and fell off the road. The underbrush had grown up so high, we did not see the drop off. I heard him struggling as he climbed back up to the road. His little head finally popped through the underbrush. I checked him closely and determined he was fine. I picked him up and carried him back to the cabin where he received a lot of love from Mom.

Now it is time to go home.

Lucky lived a long and happy life. We made many trips to our mountain cabin with him in tow. However, age and illness overcame him and he finally gave up the ghost. Anyone would have loved him and he would love them.

NOW THE FELINE WORLD EVENTS

CHAPTER FOUR

Taffy - The Abandoned One

On one of our trips to the cabin in TN, while having a cup of coffee on the porch, we heard the faint cry of a cat. My wife, her father and I heard the cry at the same time. Our front yard had not yet been maintained and the weeds were up three to four feet. As we sat there, the cry kept getting closer and closer. Finally, this little head popped up and it was a baby taffy cat. I retrieved the little fellow and opened a can of tuna and fed him. The way he ripped into that tuna was a good indication he was about to starve to death.

Here comes the conversion. We had always been dog owners. Now we have on our hands a baby kitten that was dropped off on the side of a major highway. He worked his way through the brush and brambles to meet me face to face. We cared for him every day for the 10 days we were there. Now it is time to go home. What shall we do with little Taffy? Of course! We did the right thing and packed him up and brought him home with us. He kept his name Taffy because it fit him so well.

He got adjusted to his new home really good and had the run of the house. But trouble is in the making. Our daughter-in-law just had a new baby and came out to the beach for us to see her. She was a beautiful site to see. Time came for us to eat dinner, so we took a dinner break. My daughter-in-law laid the new born on our bed while dinner was being served.

Shortly after dinner, we were playing with Taffy the cat. She was running at a high rate of speed and decided to run toward the hallway that led to the bedroom where the new born baby was sleeping. My daughter-in-law was afraid Taffy would run down and jump on the bed with the baby. She swiftly closed the hallway door and Taffy hit the door at wide open speed with his little head.

I carried Taffy to the Emergency Vet that was opened at night and they really could not determine the extent of his injury. The next day I carried him to the Vet and the Vet determine there was nothing that could be done for him and so he was put to sleep.

A good cat, still a baby, full of energy and life, was brought back to Florida only to meet his doom. Even though we only had him for a short time, we loved him and was getting attached to him. I still wonder how much fun and how long he would have lived if not for being injured.

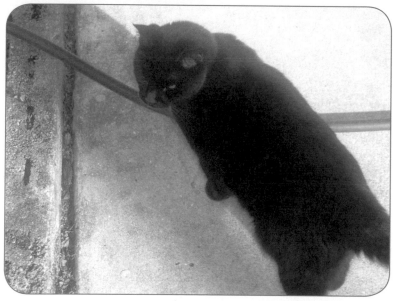

CHAPTER FIVE

Sassy – The Bipolar One

Sassy was a Calico cat that was given to me by my daughter-in-law. She was a replacement for Taffy that had a tragic accident in my home that led to his early demise. The Vet declared Sassy to be bi-polar because of her hyperactive nature. We have all heard the term the "curiosity that killed the cat" Sassy was the most curious of all the cats we ever owned.

My daughter-in-law had her spade and her front claws removed before she delivered her to me. That was a blessing indeed. As she began to settle in at her new residence, her curiosity begins to be exposed. I understand that felines are nocturnal and do all their mischief at night while the humanoids try to sleep eight uninterrupted hours. Sassy had a routine for a while of banging cabinet doors, climbing bedroom doors, and anything else that would make a racket.

The first time we traveled with Sassy was to our Mountain Cabin in Tennessee. This was a long and tiring eight-hour drive from Florida to Tennessee. Even though we had her space in the car carefully prepared for her to sleep and water to drink, it was not comforting to her. She wanted to lay in my wife's lap and breathe in the air from the A/C.

Upon arrival, my duties were to unload the auto and place everything in the rooms they belonged in. In the meantime, my wife was busy feeding and watering Sassy.

After I finished my unloading and unpacking, I wanted to check on Sassy since this is her first trip out of town and her first trip to the cabin. I could not find her anywhere. She let out a meow, and I looked up and she was on top of the kitchen cabinets next to the ceiling.

After she got through checking everything out, her favorite perch to spend the day was on the back of the sofa next to the picture window. There she could view the squirrels that came on the porch daily. She could also view the rabbits that played in the front yard daily.

We usually went somewhere on a daily basis and Sassy was perfectly content to be In charge of the cabin in our absence. When we returned everything was in its place. No strands of toilet tissue scattered throughout the cabin.

She was a good traveler. The big 18 wheelers always amazed her as they would pass on the inter-state. She could always tell when we were getting close to home. When I exited the inter-state onto the Blvd. that would lead me to the street leading to our beach house, she would begin to get restless knowing we were almost home.

When my wife and I would complete our daily tasks at home and settled down for the evening, I would watch my TV programs in the Living Room and my wife would watch her programs in the den. Sassy would become her lap top cat for a little while and then she would come in the Living Room and become a lap top cat for me.

Part of my daily routine was around 7:00 pm I would take a shower and after the shower, I would go into my computer room and spend time on the internet.

Sassy loved the computer and would go in there with me every night. She would be waiting at the bathroom door and walk with me to the computer room.

One evening, I decided not to go in the computer room. As we got to the computer room door she walked in and I continued down the hall way. She let out a real loud meow! I Turned and told her not tonight, Sassy. She ran up to me and gave me a big bite in the calve of my leg. I had a scar on my leg for a year after that.

Because she had been declawed, we kept her in the house 24/7. Her curiosity as a cat was very strong and active. With no claws she had no way of defending herself. I doubt she would be able to scale one of the palm trees in the yard to escape a predator.

However, one day the back door was left open and she found her way out. Boy, did I Panick and she panicked. She would not come to me and every time I got within reach to pick her up, she would run from me. This ordeal lasted about five minutes and finally she was wedged up next to the hurricane fence and I was able to pick her up and rescue her. She never ventured to go outside again.

She lived a long and healthy life. One evening while resting in my lap, I noticed her gasping for air. I could look at her and tell she was suffering from lack of oxygen. I decided, without hesitation and approval of my wife that the time had come for her to pass own from this life.

I carried her to the Vet the next day and he agreed that it was time for her to pass on. After all he had treated her for the last 18 or 19 years. He asked if I wanted to be present when he did the procedure and I graciously declined. He was the one that declared her to be bipolar and would not charge me a fee for putting her to sleep. She was well loved and cared for and will always be missed.

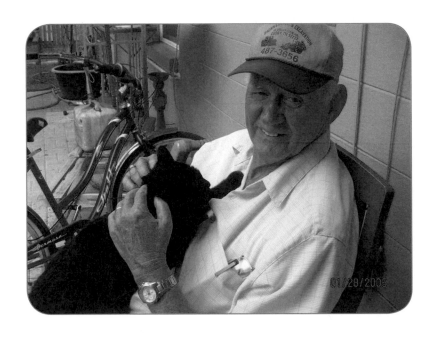

CHAPTER SIX

Foxworthy - The Sick Stranger

One morning as I was warming the car up before going to work, I saw this image going around the corner of the house that resembled a Silver Fox. I thought very little about. After all I will be late for work if I take the time to investigate. So, off to work I go.

A few days later, I go out the back door to check things out, and what do I see? Not a Silver Fox but a Burmese Feline. So, I did the right thing, I got a water hose and hosed him down so he would flee. And, that he did.

A couple of days later, he shows up again. Water hose treatment number two. This time he would not move. I got a better look at him and to me he looked sickly and I went over and picked him up. In spite of what I was doing to him, he wanted to hang out with Fritz my outside cat.

I told my wife he was not well and I filled up a feed bowl with cat food and fed him. He ate like a starving pig. He had no identification tags so I could not determine who he belonged to.

I fell in love with him instantly. Since he had no ID tag on him, I named him FOXWORTHY. I brought him inside with me and loved him and let him lay on the bed with me. He did not like lying on the bed, He really liked the outside.

He loved fritz and fritz tolerated him. When Fritz would jump the fence and leave, Foxworthy would cry for him to come back.

Because he was so thin and weak, I carried him to my Vet to have him examined. The results of the examination revealed he was dehydrated and had a severe renal infection that required IVs three times a week. The first two the Vet administered and the rest had to be done at home to relieve the financial burden.

Thanksgiving Day arrived and we fed Foxworthy some roasted turkey. He must have thought he died and went to heaven. I didn't think he would ever get full.

Giving him the IVs three days, a week became burdensome and a lot of times I hurt him injecting the needle. He was fighting it more than permitting it and we decided to discontinue them. Just a few short weeks later I discovered him trying to drink water from his bowl while lying on his side. He had gotten so week that he could not stand up to drink water. I immediately carried him to the Vet only to find out he had reached the end of his journey. So, we had the Vet to put him down.

As sick as Foxworthy was, he never complained, never was irritated and was always in a loving mood. My wife and I took his collar, that we bought for him and dated when he was put to sleep and saved it in our cedar chest.

CHAPTER SEVEN

Big Daddy - The Stolen One

Big daddy belonged to the couple in the house to our rear left.

One morning I saw him walking our fence coming my way. When he got close to me jumped from the fence and greeted me with a deep meow and what I thought was a smile. He had a tag with his name, address and phone number on it. When I saw it I was no longer concerned because he was cared for and registered and I knew where to take him if he wanted to transfer his residence.

His name on his ID was Ricky, but my wife called him Big Daddy, which really seemed to fit him better than Ricky. My wife really fell in love with him from the first time she saw him. Each day he would come over she would hold him more and started feeding him treats. It wasn't long and she started feeding him regular cat food that she fed Fritz and Foxworthy and Sassy.

I cautioned her that she was trying to steal the neighbor's cat and she kept denying it. Then one day it happened. He did not go home and did not want too. Man, was he beautiful. Big muscular white body with brown markings with big blue eyes. Who would not want him as a pet?

One day my wife tried contacting the couple to let them know that big daddy was hanging out with us. When she finally made contact with the man of the house, she found out that they were not married and the cat belonged to the female.

She finally got in touch with the female only to find out she lived in an apartment where no pets were allowed. She expressed her appreciation to my wife for her taking care of him the last few weeks and granted permission for us to keep Big Daddy as our own. I did not mind taking ownership of Big Daddy, but I was not pleased at the way she treated him and moved out of the neighborhood without finding someone to care for him. She took it for granted since my wife stole her cat, she could ease out in the middle of the night without giving us a heads up. Well, all is well that ends well.

Big Daddy was a copycat, and everything that Fritz did, Big Daddy had to do it. Fritz liked to climb on to our neighbors' roofs. Fritz was much smaller than Big Daddy and also was nimbler than Big Daddy and could get up and down quicker without assistance. What I did not know was Big Daddy was afraid of heights. Which meant he got on the roofs without any trouble but could not get down without assistance. So, Charlie my neighbor had to get out his extension ladder and climb up twice to rescue him from his roof.

In the spring time I would begin preparing my planters for flowers that would bloom during the spring and summer. I would get garden soil and potting soil and fill the planters and pots with it. One morning I was putting the food out for Big Daddy and Fritz. Guess where Big Daddy was! Spread out in the planter full of potting soil. This big beautiful, white blue-eyed feline was spread out in that planter as if this was his sleeper.

Each time I prepared anything; he automatically assumed it was for him.

One day I noticed that his nose was red and a slight nasal drip was present. My wife and I began to watch him closely. Sassy, our indoor cat was no longer living and we did not have an indoor cat.

We decided that we would bring Fritz and Big Daddy inside for their protection and we could observe them more closely. The infection began to spread and we carried him to the Vet for evaluation. After the examination came the sad news. The infection on his nose was cancer. The Vet said it was common for white cats to contract cancer of the nose. This cancer was not going to get better. We did not want to see him suffer so we had him euthanized to end his discomforts and pain.

Fritz continued on as our only pet. His story is outlined in chapter eight.

"50 YEARS OF CATS AND DOGS"

Fritz - The Project

There is a reason I call Fritz my project. He became my project from the time I first saw him until I had him put to sleep on December 12, 2021,

The project began 19 years ago, in the early hours of the morning. When I say early, I mean before day break. Back then I was a subscriber to the Florida Times Union, the local newspaper. The paper deliverer always made the delivery before day break. I liked that time of delivery because I was a working man and it gave me time to read the headlines and sports before heading off to the office.

One morning I went out to retrieve the paper and it was a real dark morning. No moon light, no street lights and no stars. I was in the process of seeking the location of the newspaper when I felt something go between my legs. Because of the darkness, I could not see anything. Whatever this was that went between my legs did not utter a sound! I began to do an Indian War Dance trying to remain silent to keep from disturbing the neighbors. Finally, I noticed this rag tag, solid black cat staring up at me. Naturally, the next thing out of my mouth was, "Where did you come from?" Of course, he remained silent.

I finally located the newspaper and proceeded to walk around the yard breathing in the early morning ocean air and checking the property as I did daily. This feline, was with me step for step. After I completed the inspection of the yard, I went inside to read the newspaper, and have my first cup of coffee of the day. I said goodby to the cat and I went inside to enjoy my coffee and newspaper. Surprisingly, the cat retreated to wherever he came from.

The next day I repeated the events of the previous day, newspaper, walked the yard, and into the house for the daily routine. This routine, with this cat, began to become a daily routine. A routine I truly looked forward to. One day, because of his color, I decided to call him Spade. He was as black as the Ace of Spades!

If I was going to form a relationship with this cat, he had to have a name to call him by. I was in no way adopting or trying to adopt this feline to be mine. I decided, if he liked company well enough to come over and walk my yard with me, he should have a name. So, out of nowhere came the utterance of Spade and it stuck for a while. Little did I know that I was becoming attached to the little fellow. He seemed to like and tolerate me and I began to look forward to him showing up for our early morning ritual. However, he never came over in the afternoon or evening.

One morning, about the break of day, Spade showed up with some friends of his. Two Calicos and another black cat. I found out quickly that group belonged to my neighbor two doors down from me. The first Calico was "Mama Cat", the second Calico was "Princess" and the black cat was "Boy Boy". I named them the "GET ALONG GANG". Same routine, when I go in, they go home. Now that is how it is supposed to be.

It came time for us to take a 10-day vacation at our mountain cabin in the Smokey Mountains. We had the inside cat, Sassy that we carried with us when we traveled to the Smokeys. After we settled in and was enjoying the setting of the cabin with snow on the ground, I mentioned to my wife that I sort of missed Spade and the get along gang. She suggested that I settle down and enjoy the peace and quiet. I took her suggestion and relaxed.

It seemed as if everywhere we went, we saw cats in the windows, on porches, crossing roads and even coming up to us for handouts. Every now and then there would be a black one like Spade. However, we did have Sassy with us and she required a lot of attention. Sassy was quite a feline herself. That was revealed in her chapter.

It seemed that this vacation time went by too fast. Now it is time for cleaning up, packing up and resting up for the eight-hour drive back home. We spent the last day of our vacation scrubbing, cleaning and sanitizing the cabin. We always do that the day before heading for home.

Early to bed and early to rise has always been my motto for traveling. We arose at 6:00 AM and departed the cabin around 6:30 AM

There are a lot of beautiful things to see traveling through the mountains of Tennessee and North Carolina. We absorbed and retained as much of that beauty as we could because it would be about four months before we would be able to return. Columbia, SC was about the halfway point to our destination and we arrived there about noon. We decided to pick up some hot lunch and go to the nearest rest area to have a picnic. It was about time to exit the automobile and stretch our legs and give our bodies a deserved rest.

After a brief break, we began the second half of our journey home. This is the first time I mentioned Spade in about three of four days. However, without thinking I asked, "do you think Spade will be glad to see me when we get home?" What brought that on? my wife asked. Nothing, I replied, just had to say something.

We arrived home around 4:30 PM. We were road weary and tired of eight hours of driving and two hours of leg stretching and taking breaks. We finally unloaded the car and put everything away. After reading the accumulated mail, we just kicked back and rested.

I did not expect to see Spade at 4:30 PM because it was not his routine. However, the get along gang showed up when I drove into the driveway.The next morning, I was retrieving my paper, anxious to be reunited with Spade. I was greeted by the get along gang. I noticed there were only three cats Two calicos and one black cat. There was Mama Cat, Princess and Boy Boy. Where is Spade, I wondered. I walked the yard as always hoping he would catch up soon. Spade never showed up. I decided to go in for coffee and read the newspaper and head off to work as was the normal routine for me.

The work day was quite pleasant for being gone for two weeks. Everyone seemed to be glad to see me and throughout the day they kept bringing me up to speed on everything. The day also passed pretty quickly for the first day back. I was so looking forward to getting home so as to reunite with Spade. The Monday afternoon traffic seemed to be extra heavy going home. Even though it seemed like it was taking me longer to get home this day, it was the normal time of travel.

I anxiously dismounted from the car expecting to be greeted by Spade. That did not happen! What a disappointment that was. As was the custom, my wife came out to greet me and I asked her if she had seen Spade anytime during the day.

Her answer was no. She then said, "I was not really looking for him." With that I went inside for a hot meal, catch up on the news and relax for the remainder of the day.

It's Tuesday morning and the routine begins again. I retrieve my newspaper, the get along gang greets me, and no Spade! I now begin to think something bad has happened to my morning greeter. My heart begins to race within me! I could not enjoy the reading the newspaper and I waited until I got to the office to have coffee.

I have always been a productive worker, so I did not let my feelings interfere with my duties. All day I tried to come up with a plan to locate Spade. One thought was to contact the Humane Society to see if someone had dropped him off there.

Finally! Spade returns! After about three days, I hear this cat moaning at a distance. The day was early, overcast with a slight drizzle of rain. The moaning kept getting closer, and closer and BINGO, there he was! The long-lost feline.

The happiness turned into sadness when he finally made it to me. I picked him up to love him and I did not like what I saw. HIs bottom jaw was broken and hanging down, his left eye was damaged and he had a terrible laceration under his left front leg. His condition was so bad that it struck me emotionally and tears came into my eyes.

I rushed Spade to the Vet. I thought, in his condition, they would put him to sleep. He was not my cat and I did not know who he belonged to. At the time of registering him, he had to have a name. At this time, I thought he was a she, so I named him Queen. The Vet said he could not be a queen because he was a male, so I name him King.

I explained to the Vet that this was not my cat and I did not know who his owner was. I also explained to the Vet I had very little money myself, but something had to be done to give him relief from his suffering. The Vet asked me to leave him there for evaluation and he would do something.

Around 4:30 PM, the Vet called me to let me know that my cat was ready for pickup. The Vet's office was only 15 minutes from where I was, but I think I shortened that time.

The Vet did a great job on King. He reset his Jaw and stitched the laceration under his leg. His prognosis was to keep him isolated from other animals for about six weeks to allow his jaw to completely heal.

We have a 12'X10' wooden shed behind our house we use for a laundry room. The shed was fully wired with overhead lights. There are four double plugs for additional support for electronic appliances. I put a comfortable chair in there for me to sit and hold him. I sat there and fed him until he could eat on his own.

We decided to adopt him since I had to pay $200.00 to bail him out from the Vet. Now we decided to give him a name that he could live and die with, "FRITZ". That was my father-in-law's nick name.

Fritz healed up with emotional scars left from whatever happened to him. I don't know if he was hit by a big truck, attacked by a big dog, or ran into a moving lawn mower. I do know each day the refuse company would come and collect the garbage; he would retreat to the back of the house and stay there until complete quietness would return. Any loud noise would cause him to react that way.

FRITZ AND THE CROWS

One day while holding Fritz in my lap, I tuned in YouTube to learn a lot about Crows. The program I was watching showed how Crows would get and eat their food. There was a lot of activity during this showing with about six Crows. This excited Fritz and he exited my lap and jumped on the TV stand to interact with the Crows. When they would fly off and disappear, he would walk behind the TV to see if they were there. We did this for about three or four days and finally he figured out that he could not make contact with them and he quit looking for them.

FRITZ AND THE SPARROWS

The most amazing thing Fritz ever did was when he had an encounter with a Sparrow.

One spring day, my wife, Fritz and me were in the shed where we had our washer and dryer. The shed door was open and a sparrow flew in and perched in the rafters. He would fly from one rafter to another. Fritz was in the room at the time and noticed the sparrow flying around trying to find a way out. He climbed into the rafters to assist the bird or destroy it. He finally caught the Sparrow in flight with his mouth. I coaxed Fritz to bring the Sparrow to me. He slowly climbed down to me and as I reached out to get the Sparrow, Fritz released him too soon and he flew back into the rafters. Fritz, once again returned to the rafters and retrieved the bird for the second time. This time we were successful and the bird was released to the outside and freedom.

What was more amazing is the next spring it happened again! A sparrow flew into the shed, went into the rafters and perched there. Fritz climbed into the rafters and once again caught the sparrow by mouth in midair and brought it down to me. He was successful on the first try releasing the bird to me and I released him to the outside and freedom

Because of his traumatic experience when he was a young cat, he never enjoyed being a Kitten. He did not have the urge to play with toys like most kittens growing into adulthood. He had his moments but not very often. He mostly was an outside cat during the day. At night I would put him in the shed with a fan blowing in the summer and a heater in the winter. For about 19 years I worried, loved and cared for him.

One day he was acting a little strange and did not seem to be himself. I carried him to the Vet and the examination revealed he had lung cancer. We decided to bring him inside and convert him to be an inside cat. It took him awhile to adjust to the change but finally he began to manage it very well.

After about four years, the lung cancer spread and he developed fluid around his heart. Because of this condition it effected his breathing. We decided after 19 years it would be best to have him put to sleep. The Vet agreed that was the best decision.

Because of our ages, we decided Fritz was and will be our last pet. The emotional strain is too much. We always get closely attached to our pets and it hurts too much emotionally.

Fritz did not have a pedigree. However, he was a project the whole time he lived. Sometimes it was mentally painful and sometimes it was joyful. To me he was the most loyal animal I ever owned. I will forever remember him and miss the mornings of retrieving my newspaper and having him to greet me.

EVERY PET LOVER SHOULD HAVE A FRITZ AS A PROJECT.

Printed in the United States
by Baker & Taylor Publisher Services